ANIMAL
Spot-the-Differences

Fran Newman-D'Amico

Dover Publications, Inc.
Mineola, New York

Bibliographical Note

Animal Spot-the-Differences is a new work, first published by
Dover Publications, Inc., in 2007.

International Standard Book Number
ISBN-13: 978-0-486-45649-2
ISBN-10: 0-486-45649-8

Manufactured in the United States by Courier Corporation
45649808   2014
www.doverpublications.com

Note

Welcome to a fun little book that is filled with animals of all sorts—you'll find frogs on a lily pad, doggie pals, hatching chicks, a skateboard-riding monkey, and many more adorable creatures!

To do the spot-the-differences activities, first look carefully at each left-hand page. The page facing it on the right looks just the same—but it's not! Some things have changed, and it's up to you to spot all of the things that are different. As you find each one, draw a circle around it.

Try to finish the activities on your own. You can check your answers in the Solutions section, which begins on page 58. When you are done, have even more fun by coloring in the pages with crayons, markers, or colored pencils. Remember to look carefully!

Willy and Wally are relaxing on a lily pad. Willy is trying to catch a spider.

4

Now look! There are 5 things that are different in the picture. Find and circle all of them.

The Tortoise Triplets are celebrating their team's win.

What's different in the picture? Find and circle 6 things that have changed.

Fernando always brushes his teeth before he goes to bed.

Look again. What is different in the picture? Circle the
3 things that are different.

Louise loves to jump rope. It's her favorite type of exercise!

What's different? Look carefully and circle 4 things
that have changed in the picture.

Martin is reading a book about cheese. He is quite an expert!

Now the picture looks different. Find and circle 4 things that have changed.

Maria has a birthday present for Stan the Snowman.

Take another look at the picture. Find 5 things that are different and circle them.

Rita Robin is getting dinner ready for her hungry family.

16

There are 3 things different in the picture. Find the changes and circle all of them.

Polly and Patrick are snug in their den for the winter.

The picture looks the same, but 3 things have changed.
Circle the things that are different.

19

These doggie pals are out for a drive.

Now look at the picture. There are 5 differences. Find and circle them all.

Fluffy is enjoying her walk. She doesn't mind the rain at all.

Here's Fluffy, but the picture isn't the same. Find and circle the 4 things that make it different.

Lulu is so excited to see her chicks hatching!

Now the picture looks different. Can you find and circle the 4 things that have changed?

Thomas is having so much fun riding his sled in the snow.

The picture looks the same, but it isn't. Find and circle the 4 things that make it different.

Many different creatures live together in the sea.

Some parts of this underwater picture have changed.
Circle the 4 things that are different.

It's a great day for a walk. Samantha says a big "Hello" to her friends.

30

What's different in the picture? Find and circle the 4 things that have changed.

Chuck is on his way home from a fishing trip.

Look at the picture again. Circle the 5 things that make it different from the other picture.

Pinky needs a bath after rolling in the mud in the barnyard!

34

This picture is different from the other one. Circle the 4 things that have changed.

Harold is trying out his new scooter. Look at him go!

Look carefully at the picture. Can you find and circle the 4 things that make it different?

Wanda is on her way to see her grandparents. She'll get there faster on her skis.

38

The picture of Wanda has changed. Look for the 4 things that are different and circle them.

Paul and Paula Panda could chew on tasty bamboo
all day.

What's different in this picture of Paul and Paula?
Circle the 4 things that have changed.

41

Here's Emily—she's a ballet dancer with the circus.

This picture of Emily looks the same, but it's not. Find and circle the 5 things that make it different.

Ricky and Taffy are having a nice chat in the birdbath.

Look again! The picture has changed. Circle the 4 things that make it different.

Lester is putting the finishing touches on his painting.

What's different in the picture of Lester and his painting? Find and circle the 4 changes.

Sylvester looks a bit silly in his wool hat, but it keeps him warm.

Can you spot the 4 things that are different in the picture? Circle them all.

You could reach those delicious coconuts if you were
as tall as Alvin!

50

Alvin's still here, but 4 things have changed in the picture. Circle all 4 things.

These animal friends are getting together for an afternoon chat.

52

Look carefully. Can you find and circle the 4 things that are different?

The baby ducklings are ready for their first swim.

This picture looks different, doesn't it? Find and circle the 4 things that have changed.

Nicky is coming in for a landing. He steers clear of the mountain and trees.

56

Here's Nicky, but look carefully and you will find 5 things that have changed. Circle them all.

Solutions

page 5

page 7

page 9

page 11

page 13

page 15

page 17

page 19

page 21

page 23

page 25

page 27

page 29

page 31

page 33

page 35

page 37

page 39

page 41

page 43

page 45

page 47

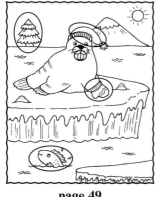

page 49

page 51

page 53

page 55

page 57